WINE, WOMEN, WARREN, AND SKIS
By
WARREN A. MILLER
(He drew the pictures, too)

Published by
Goldfinkle, Masowitch, Kloppenboig, & O'Brien
Publishers to his late Majesty, King George XIII
P.O. Box 350, Deer Harbor, Washington 98243

In 1956 when the free program I published for the personal appearance showings of my latest ski film needed some written copy, I wrote a story about living in the parking lot at Sun Valley Idea for eighteen cents a day during the winter of 1946/47. When the printer got finished setting the type, he had some extra room for another paragraph, so I wrote the following: **"To reserve your copy of Wine, Women, Warren & Skis at the pre-publication discount price of $2.00, mail me a penny postcard with your name and address and, when the book is published, I will mail your copy C.O.D."**

Six hundred and thirty two people mailed me two dollars!

I thought I was rich!

The following year, the title of the story in that year's ski film program was **"GOOD GRIEF MORE EXCERPTS."** That winter 1119 people mailed me their two dollars. During that time I was personally narrating the film in over a hundred different cites, traveling to all of the ski resorts to get the footage for the following winter, editing the film, putting together the musical score, soliciting ski club bookings, writing the script, and sleeping on Greyhound busses more nights than I care to remember.

In the spring when the book had not been written and mailed out, irate customers started to ask for their two dollars back. I had already spent all of their money for film and travel, so late in the summer I sat down at a manual typewriter and without spell check or anyone to correct the punctuation, dangling participles, or politically incorrect statements, I typed, cut, and pasted the book together and then timed the self-publication release date so it would be delivered one week before the first showing of the 1958 film. I knew I could sell the book personally from the theater stage for $2.00 and make a dollar a book profit. I paid the printer on time, and it is now forty-six years and five more books later. So join me back in the Sun Valley parking lot one year before I bought a riverfront lot in nearby Ketchum for $350.00., and pardon any politically incorrect foibles, grammar or punctuation mistakes that are causing my 9th grade English teacher to rollover in her grave.

Warren Miller

DEDICATION

To Miss Abigail Nicelunchowski, inventor of the oyster cracker. Without whose foresight in offering vitamin enriched oyster crackers to the Union Pacific Railroad for their Sun Valley Idaho operation, I might never have survived the terrible winter of 1946. Good luck to you, Miss Abigail Nicelunchowski, wherever you are.

Miss Abigail Nicelunchowski

1912 - 1963

A FROSTBITTEN SAGA OF FORGED LIFT TICKETS, EMPTY KETCHUP BOTTLES, AND OLD RABBIT CARCASSES

FEATURING

WARD BAKER

WARREN MILLER

Chamonix France. March 1988

L'Aiguille du Midi looms ominously above us as we glide silently through the sky three thousand feet above the jagged rocks below. In the telecabin in which we are riding everyone speaks in whispers through fear that the two mile long cable will break if we talk too loud. In the corner an elderly woman rides skyward to serve food in the restaurant at the top. Beside me the subdued discussion of three Italian mountaineers intent on making the first spring ascent of the east face of Mt. Blanc murmurs on. Behind me a guide is patiently explaining in halting English to his four American customers that le Mír de Glace is indeed a ski run of over eight miles on snow and ice that in places is over a thousand feet deep. For my wife and I, this is a thrill that will not be soon forgotten. It has been a long uphill climb. But most of it has been easy because my life has been downhill all the way. Fifty years now, since I first saw a skier make a turn in the San Bernadino Mountains near Los Angeles. Fifty years of producing ski films and living out of suitcases, traveling all over the world while skiing on almost every hill in the world that has a ski lift.

The telecabin is slowing down for the top terminal, its' motion guided by some unseen engineer down in the bowels of the machinery that powered us up here. Now empty, the telecabin departs and swings gently on it's sheaves as it drops through space towards the lower terminal. We turn and grope our way through the dark tunnels toward the restaurant carved out of solid rock, there to have a warm cup of tea, before our descent on skis.

As I sit here waiting for the scalding hot tea to brew, a strange feeling has come over me. A feeling of security yet desire. A desire to look back over the route that brought me here. How can I explain a trip of millions of miles? How did it start? Where did it start? When?

To find the answers to these questions I walked across the room and gazed out through spaces in the frost covered windows. Gazed out and down, down and back, back many years to the end of World War Two. Back to when I was sunk in Hurricane Betsy that roared across the South Pacific. Back to when I was ordered back to the States for temporary duty to wait for the outfitting of another ship. Back to when I had hair.

Images of the first six months and five thousand miles of the thirty nine year trip came flowing back over me.

DONNER PASS, 1945

I was temporarily stationed in San Francisco. It was December 1945 and I was returning from a three day pass in Reno.

My Ensign brass, slightly tarnished from forty seven days of sea duty still gleamed against the falling snow. The windshield wipers had years ago reached their peak of efficiency. Now they barely slurped back and forth in time to the spasmodic wheezing of my already ancient 1937 Buick. I was driving over Donner Summit enroute back to the Naval Base. The smoothness of my prewar tires finally forced me to pay twentyninefifty for eleven pounds of baling wire and rope in a bag labeled "skid chains." The only man in town who knew how to put them on, charged a dollar an hour for his time and eight dollars an hour for his specially designed tools.

Two hours later, they were ready to roll and I did. The car now lurched, slipped and boiled its way up towards the summit. After negotiating Death Curve sideways and Corkscrew Canyon backwards, the car slid once more, hiccuped twice and groundlooped into a snowbank. As I settled back waiting to be rescued, the snow drifted through the cracks in my convertible top. Cracks? They were big holes. I looked out of the largest hole and there on the nearby hillside gaily garbed girls and handsome men dipped and darted in what seemed to me a suicidal dance. They would hurtle down the hill at a frightening speed only to stop at the last instant and grab a piece of rope that would haul them skyward again.

It was about the tenth time I watched a trio of carefree girls grab the rope and go up, that I noticed something strange about them. Their right arm was seven inches longer than their left. A malady, I was to find out later, that is not uncommon among guests at resorts featuring this type of uphill conveyance.

Being of sound mind ?? and nosey by nature I decided to investigate this method of limb stretching.

"Rope Tow," the ancient one answered as he took my thirtynine dollars for three quarts of what, he told me, was home made anti-freeze. Two hours later I had a room in the hotel, a quart and a half of the anti-freeze in the radiator and a quart and half of it on the dresser to have with dinner, and a pair of rented ski boots.

"The toes are turned up on the end in case your skis fall off," the man said. To me the ski poles looked like they came from China with a rug wrapped around them but the skis had genuine metal edges.

With a two dollar rope tow ticket stapled to my Navy jacket I started across the railroad tracks towards the tinkling laughter that drifted across the new fallen snow.

I forgot to rent a train schedule. By the time I did my version of a kickturn, the 8:45 out of Reno cut off the tip of one ski, the tail of the other and cut my poles in half which was O.K. because I could now reach the handles without standing on my tippytoes.

My blood, thinned by a tour of tropical duty, offered about as much warmth as a hot water bottle to an elephant with a head cold. This together with my near accident made me hurry the rest of the way to the rope tow. Actually, I floundered terror stricken.

"Rope Tow," to quote one of our leading ski writers, "Man's most economical way to get more people up

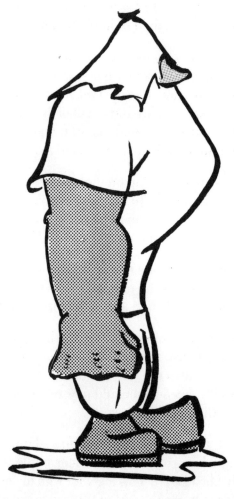

"The closest left-handed rope tow is in Chile"

more hills, in less time, than with any other means of uphill transportation yet invented." In all fairness to the clothing manufacturers they should have a left handed rope tow, here and there, so that people could stretch the other arm a little now and then. My first day on the rope tow we will forget. By nightfall I looked like a prisoner of Ghengis Khan after fourteen hours on the rack.

That night the thermometer dropped to seventeen below zero. I found the home brewed antifreeze I had purchased was the wrong vintage for cars. It made no difference, however, since I had figured out that General Motors had enough sense to make engines so they would withstand a little cold. Two hundred and eighty dollars and a new engine later I found out that the General wasn't as smart as he had led everyone to believe.

TIME MOVES ON AND WE SKIP FORWARD TO CHRISTMAS 1945

While fulfilling my obligations of overseas duty someone had goofed and I was sunk in a Hurricane. "Routine", I think the Board of Inquiry called it. With this survival leave due me, together with my recent Donner Summit survival, I packed my new skis and started for Yosemite. Well, the skis were NEARLY new anyway. I had bought a pair of boots, bindings and skis and poles from a fellow who had heart trouble above three thousand feet. Unable to find any snow below that altitude in California, he had reluctantly parted with them and their genuine prewar high speed, brass edges for twenty six dollars.

YOSEMITE 1945

Cold powder snow. I rode up on the lift and walked

*". . .and walked down with wads of it
glued to the bottom of my skis."*

down the hill with wads of snow glued to the bottom of my skis. The closest I had ever been to powder before was on my lapels at a dance hall in Miami, Florida. The local ski pro set me straight. "Wrong Wax".

Have you ever tried to remove bubble gum from a sidewalk?

That night I thought, "Gasoline works on cold bubble-gum. Why not on this klister wax that was as sticky as bubblegum ?"

As I sat in my cabin, skis laying on the bed, I began to remove the wads of wax with a gasoline soaked rag. As each piece of towel soaked up the wax, I would throw it in the wood stove that heated the cabin.

"Can't have gasoline soaked rags lying around. Spontaneous combustion you know."

Seventeen rags later the cabin got so hot I had to take off one of my sweaters. Another rag another sweater. Off with my parka, off with my T-shirt, off with my long johns, and then it came to me. Open the door and let some cool air in. I did. As I stood there looking into the faces of about two hundred people, the sky was red in the west. In fact, it was red in the east, and straight up too. Flames, fortythree feet high, were shooting out of my cabin chimmney and had already set fire to three trees, a nearby house trailer, and the district rangers convertible, and I was standing there in my jockey shorts.

The next morning the judge granted me some time off because of my Navy Campaign Bars. (Marksmanship, Pacific Theatre, Good Conduct, and one little bitty green one for not missing class for a month.)

By 10:30 the next morning my fire building fame had spread to the lift crew. They made me climb. I climbed and climbed and climbed. Seventeen agonizing climbs up the big hill and seventeen learn-to-turn descents later it was lunch time. My frozen feet needed warming up. I took off my boots and socks. I couldn't have covered my blisters with a whole Blue Jay. Much less a corn plaster. So I packed my skis, bandaged my feet, untaped my knee, and reluctantly headed back to Navy Duty.

NEW YEARS EVE. MY LEAVE WAS UP.

Enroute to San Diego I stopped off at Malibu to ride my surfboard before settling down to the monotony of Navy life. I reported aboard ship at 23:55 (almost midnight) only to stand around while everyone drank yet another toast to the New Year. Next morning, with my blisters so full of sand I couldn't wear shoes, my necktie still in the fireplace in Yosemite, I stood with officer's hat in hand, barefooted, hitchiking back to the beach to recover from my Christmas leave.

Finally, to get squared away with the Navy, I again drew temporary duty in San Francisco. The War was over now and the only reason for temporary duty was so

my body would be available, on short notice, to ship west if they had an order for one of my particular dimensions. Being a junior officer I was sure to get duty at some long forgotten outpost in the Pacific like Funafuti, Guadalcanal, or Tulagi. Once there my duties would probably be to keep the beer cold, see that the grass didn't get too long in front of the BOQ, and try and keep the enlisted men from getting a positive Wasserman.

The young lady that handled my orders, upon my arrival in San Francisco was very pleasant company at dinner a few evenings later. Nine dinners later my orders somehow got buried in the bottom drawer. Instead of reporting every morning for muster, I just phoned her to see if my orders had come in. Six phone calls later I started calling her from Yosemite.

"No orders today."

I figured each day was my last day so I would ski like the snow was going to melt forever. Each night was, of course, my last night in Yosemite, so I would go to a farewell party. Fortynine farewell parties later, I was tired. I now knew the difference between a parallel christie on ice and bourbon over ice, a broken rib and a cracked one, torn cartilage and a broken ankle, tight sweaters and why girls wear gloves over wedding rings.

ORDERS TO GUAM

The war had been over for almost a year now and everyone was counting the days to earn enough points to get mustered out. I was assigned to an obsolete type ship that had been tied to the dock so long you could walk all the way around it on the piles of empty beer cans and debris that had been tossed over the side. They had

"*I took over the piloting of this vehicle of death.*"

ruined one of the engines two years before when a mechanic had pumped the oil out and put in salt water instead. The crew had their own jeep, a truck, and a three wheeled motorcycle. I'd never ridden a motorcycle in my life, but since I outranked the transportation officer by three days I took over the piloting of this vehicle of death. For the first eight or ten days aboard ship I spent every moment driving from one end of the island to the other on the three wheeler. Nights out under the stars at an out of the way movie house; trips to native villages; swimming at magnificent beaches.

One day I got back early from one of my drives to see the crew playing football on the dock. Asphalt field, fifty gallon drums for goals, the ocean on one side for an out of bounds, and a metal quonset hut for the other.

They played a rough, tough, brand of football as I climbed up from out of bounds. The first play, they had me run around end and I forgot to come back. The swim would have been nice but the tide was out and I landed head first in the leavings from lunch. From then on I ran like greased lightning. No one could grab ahold of me. I was covered with eighteen pounds of melted fat I had fallen into. I was the first officer of the ship to ever play football with the enlisted men, and of course, in regular Navy circles that is strictly forbidden. By sundown, sick bay was half full of guys who had tried to get in the act of half massacring a well oiled officer. Our side lost 137 to 96.

I was confined to my quarters for conduct unbecoming an officer and a gentleman. When my confinement was up I was transferred to another ship.

BIRD DOG PATROL

Our job was to go out to some fixed point in the Pacific and sit there for twenty eight days. If an airplane went down we were supposed to find it. By now, any sailor with any seniority at all had enough points to get on a ship for home and be discharged. Ours was the motliest array of non sailors you can imagine. Most of them, like myself, didn't know a depth charge from a Danforth anchor. Somehow we got the ship underway and set out for a point midway between Eniwetok and Guam. For the next twenty eight days we steamed around in a two mile radius circle. Twelve hours clockwise and twelve hours counter clockwise.

One afternoon our ship slowly took a definite port list. After eating lunch on an extreme angle the skipper phoned the engine room, "no flooding" phoned the bridge, "sea calm." Finally he came topside and there, three crewmen and myself had plugged up the scuppers of a 40MM gun tub, filled it with water and had a private swimming pool about twenty feet in diameter. We had filled it with water about four feet deep and were climbing up and diving off of the gun barrels. This was mixed up with swimming round and round the gun in ever decreasing left turns until we were dizzy.

The skipper sounded "General Quarters." Everyone raced to their battle stations. But as they ran by the midship gun tub they thought we were awash and sinking. "Abandon ship. Man the port lifeboats." This caused the ship to list even further to port and the water began to pour out of our pool, across the deck, over a coaming, and down into the wardroom. The sudden rush of four or five inches of water into the wardroom broke up a poker game that had been in continuous operation for one hundred and eighty nine days.

War is Hell.

Half way through this "bird dog patrol" my points were enough so I was eligible for discharge which meant nothing until we got off of patrol. Nineteen more days. That night an electrican mate spilled a cup of coffee in our radar set so we could no longer watch for airplanes effectively. COMCINCPAC let us in off of patrol. In the meantime the skipper had also gotten enough points and turned over his command to the next ranking officer. Fresh out of school, the new skipper was suddenly in charge of one hundred and thirty four men who cared less about the war than he did. We steamed into Eniwetok at flank speed and requested permission to take on water.

"Granted."

Hard right rudder and over to the water barge. It soon became agonizingly clear that our new skipper didn't know a rudder command from a breeches buoy as he eased into the water barge at eight knots and sliced a hole in the side of it you could drive a truck into.

"Full speed astern."

We backed off and brought the barge with us. Along with the men on it, their tattoos, two dogs, three cats, and a monkey who were all scrambling for their lives. Unable to hear their screams in the confusion they began to frantically signal with semaphore flags. The only man left aboard our ship who could read semaphore was a motor mechanic in charge of engine signals below.

"To hell with the engines, get that man up here !"

"They say, if we back off they will sink."

"Full speed ahead then. Have them cast off their bow and stern anchors and we'll push them into shallow water."

A ship of our size needed a lot more water to float in than the barge. About four feet to be exact. We ran aground while there was still three feet of water under the barge. They had about a foot or so of freeboard. As our ship ground to a stop the barge slowly slid away from us and settled until only a couple of valves and part of the aft cabin was visible. Atop the cabin sat the crew, their dogs, cats, monkey, and a hundred and eightyseven rats. The only survivors of our "Action in the Pacific."

Two weeks later I ambled down Market Street, my mustering out pay in my clammy little fist. Train ticket. Los Angeles. Home, beach, swim, ride a surfboard, war stories, girls, and then the days began to get cold. Sitting on the beach I began to reminisce, with fascinated awe, about all of the pretty girls that would soon be gliding gracefully down the slopes. The thrill of cartwheeling at high speed down a steep hill. The patient waiting in lift lines as you calculate what that last run just cost you in dollars per lineal foot of snow traveled.

"That's for me."

ENTER WARD BAKER

An unemployed fisherman from Manhattan Beach California.

Ward and I put some money together and bought a house trailer. Only eight feet long and four feet high, it contained a stove, sink, a double bed, and an ice box. Three weeks later a hardy band of pioneers, two to be exact, headed east towards Salt Lake City and Alta. Trailing out behind my ancient Buick, the trailer looked like a deep freeze version of Grapes of Wrath that had taken the wrong turn out of Dallas. We were loaded down with second hand skis, army surplus sleeping bags and the remains of three goats that Ward had shot on Catalina Island. We were hard put to keep the car in front of the smells that kept following us. Actually the goats weren't smelly if you like dead goats. It was the sixty pounds of mackerel that we brought along that kind of got us down. Each night as we bedded down, we would remove the dry ice, the goat meat, and mackerel from our sleeping bags and insert our bodies instead.

Two hundred and eighty seven miles and three days later, Las Vegas. The knock in the engine began to get louder than the flapping of our canvas convertible roof. As we drove by the Frontier the engine sounded like the First Marine Division assualt on Iwo Jima. Two miles later the engine gave up completely and we coasted into the sanctuary of a combination gas station, motel, trailer park, swimming pool, gambling hall, restaurant, miniature golf course, laundromat, pool hall, garage, night club type of place that was so typical of Las Vegas. We let the engine knock a bit longer for the garage attendant to diagnose. He turned up his hearing aid so he could hear

A deep-freeze version of "The Grapes of Wrath."

the knock over the din of the hotel guests screaming to "shut off that damn noise", and with rare wisdom for a man of his I.Q. he said, "engine trouble".

He was right.

We found a place to park and mooching a few tools, we dismantled the engine. Wrecked it, would be more truthful. The trouble finally located, we made a trip through half a dozen junk yards and luckily found a part that matched the broken one in our engine.

By now, the light rain had turned to heavy snow. Working outside, we finally had the engine ready to put back together. It looked like a chocolate cake with vanilla icing. We looked like a couple of fellas' that had just swam a slow quarter mile in a Standard Oil storage tank after covering ourselves with goat hair and mackerel scales.

In our eight foot trailer, we had no heat, water, or anything else for that matter. We did have some slightly ripe mackerel and goat meat. How to get clean?

A movie? . . . For sixty-five cents we could get warm in the lobby, wash up in the men's room and and see Sophia Glockenheim in 3D. Since we were too dirty to gain admittance, we dug out some army surplus ponchos we had brought along. Camouflaged, like Marines at Guadalcanal, we ambled down the street into the glitter and swank of Las Vegas. Actually, we looked more like a Marine Supply Corps mistake. Amid the jibes of "Halloween's over", we paid our sixty five cents and fumbled our way to some seats. The heat of the theater finally began to invade our bodies and so the ponchos came off. We were grease and grime from head to foot. We had, we thought, wisely decided to wait until later to wash up.

Camouflaged like Marines at Guadacanal

About the time we got warm enough to vaporize the gasoline-oil-mackerel-goat odor, the first picture ended. Intermission. The lights went up and we felt as conspicuous and smelly as a skunk at a cat show. Have you ever tried to hide in a front row center seat camouflaged with a Marine surplus poncho?

Two days later, Ward somehow managed to finally reassemble the engine of the ancient Buick with only eighteen pounds of parts left over. With the talent of many years of working on Model A Fords, this was par for the course. He put the eighteen pounds of left over parts in an old duffle bag, rubbed a little grease on his left ear, put a 5/8th socket wrench in his shirt pocket for good luck, faced the southeast, counted to nineteen by halves, climbed into the car and stepped on the starter. It didn't!

He then ran four times, counterclockwise, around the car, lifted up the hood, put it down again, climbed in, stepped on the starter and it did. Why? He turned on the key. It then gave a couple spasmodic coughs, a few burps, and started purring like a laryngetic lion. We shoveled the tools in on top of the left over parts, dumped them into the back seat for additional ballast, lashed the skis down again, and were off like a herd of turtles, as a driving blizzard roared down on us.

On the ninth day, we broke our travel record by traveling 183 miles in fourteen hours. At dusk, I spotted a gigantic sign so large it would hardly fit into our souvenir bag. "Alta, 12 MILES." Following the arrows it was up hill all the way. Somehow, the ancient baling wire chains held together as Ward and I took turns pushing and driving. Finally, when the road went no further, and the snow

That night the thermometer dropped to eleven below.

*Getting dressed in the trailer was like trying to
play a trombone in a deep-freeze.*

was eight feet deep on three sides of the car, like Brigham Young, Ward said:

"This is the place."

It was.

We dug down through the snow until we could get the door of the trailer open, climbed in, removed a portion of our clothes and got into bed. Climbed out of bed, removed what was left of the frozen mackerel and climbed back in.

That night the thermometer dropped to eleven below zero causing a rather peculiar atmospheric phenomenom. Our breath would condense, freeze, and then cling to the ceiling and walls. As the frozen vapor built up it finally got to a point where no more would stick to the ceiling and it would come drifting back down in the form of snow. In the morning, we woke up with four inches of snow inside the trailer.

We woke up early to the roar of the rotary snowplow as it came within one and seven-eighths inches of our trailer wheels and only six inches from our heads. This was followed by a bulldozer that removed the rear fender from our car and was about to mill around on the roof of the trailer when the driver veered off because of the muffled screams he heard coming from under the snow. Us.

Getting dressed inside the trailer was a big problem. The trailer being only four feet high and four feet wide, standing up was impossible. The best comparison I can give you is to remove all of the food from your deep freeze, put your clothes and sleeping bag in and climb in and shut the lid. When the alarm goes off the following morning try to put your frozen clothes on without break-ing them or opening the lid.

Boots are a real problem. Mine froze so hard one night I broke the tongue off the following morning. Came in handy a week later as a tire iron.

Once you climb into your frozen clothes and snap, crackle, and pop out of the trailer, you go to the back and start up the stove. Put on a pan, fill it up with icicles to melt and you are ready. Get the milk out of the ice box, chip away a chunk or two with the ice pick, and get ready to put it on the oatmeal once that is cooked. Water boil-ing, oatmeal cooking, fingers freezing, toes frozen, the frozen milk is slowly thawed out. It took so long for the hot oatmeal to thaw out the frozen milk, they both reached a semi-frozen condition at the same time. If you waited another minute and a half the whole bowl of oatmeal could be eaten like a popsicle.

An all day lift ticket in 1946 was $2.50. This of course was completely out of our budget unless we wanted to push the ancient Buick back home. We spent the first few days climbing the hill and getting used to skiing so far back east. We became acquainted with some of the em-ployees and located a weekend job in one of the lodges. The lift line was extremely long on Saturdays and Sun-days so Ward and I didn't mind cooking hamburgers. We each got $5.00 a day and all we could eat. We both cooked a lot more hamburgers than we had orders for and visited the trailer several times during the weekend. The ten dollars we each earned paid for our lifts for four days during the week and the hamburgers offered a welcome change of diet from goat meat mackerel. All told our vacation at Alta, aside from Ace bandages and liniment, cost only $2.50 a week.

Finally, running out of goat meat and running low on money we left for Los Angeles. The trip home was boring except for the three hitch hikers we picked up in Las Vegas. They said they had gotten fired from their jobs and were enroute to Los Angeles to stay. I thought it odd that three hitch hikers would have only one small suitcase between them.

"Oh, it has all of our clothes and costumes in it."

"And why did you get fired from your jobs?"

"Our 'G' strings were too small."

And Los Angeles is three hundred miles from Las Vegas.

THANKSGIVING AT HOME

We really had alot to be thankful for. We had already skied for three weeks and were still alive after driving three hundred miles from Las Vegas in three hours and eleven minutes.

During this time, I was romancing a girl whose father owned a ski resort in Arizona. This enabled us to get a job there for the rest of the winter. We had it figured out so we could work in the afternoon on the rope tow, go to school in the morning and ski in between. Unfortunately, the ancient Buick fell apart just as I picked up Ward for the journey South. Best estimate I could get from the garage that it broke down in front of was $438.00 for a new engine and an etc. (An "etc." was what cost so much. The new engine was from a Mark Thirteen Sherman Tank and available at any army surplus store for $27.95.)

*We flipped to see who would hitchhike and
who would drive. I lost . . .*

Fortunately, Ward had a car that ran, although it was of an even more extreme vintage. I left my car in the garage and we dumped all our gear into his. Clothes, skis, boots. food, stove, camera gear, some frozen mackerel, goat meat, dry ice, and some old abalone shells to trade with the Indians. By the time we got our overcoats, flight boots, and cold weather hats on, we both tried to get into the front seat of his Model A Ford. Didn't fit. We flipped to see who would hitch hike and who would drive. I lost and Ward hitch hiked and beat me there by four and a half days.

The drive was routine. That is, if you call almost getting killed twice by a horse routine. The first time, I was asleep by the side of the road near Las Vegas and awoke to the hot breath and slurping of what sounded like a fire-eating monster. I raised my eyelids a bit and looked into what resembled a gigantic set to false teeth. They belonged to a horse who had leaned over the fence I was sleeping next to and was slowly inhaling the feathers from a hole in my down sleeping bag.

The other horse that almost killed me was just out of Hackberry, Arizona. Low on gas and coasting downhill at about 65 mph, with the lights off (due to an oversight on Ward's part). They wouldn't work unless the motor was running and the car was in second gear. Around a corner. There, in the headlights of an oncoming Diesel truck was silhoutted the biggest horse I had ever seen. Scared by the roar of the truck and sensing something ominously approaching him from the other direction (me), he was torn between self preservation and making a statistic out of me. I ducked my head, swerved, went off the road and through a public camp ground. The Ford ground to a halt after knocking over three picnic tables, a barbecue pit, and wound up nestled half way between the men's outhouse and second base. By this time, the horse had met a rather ignominious end by being branded by the front bumper of a Route "66" semi-truck and trailer.

By the gray light of dawn, I got out the car backed out of the field, rearranged all of the stuff so I could shift gears and coughed and sputtered my way noisily into Chloride, Arizona.

When I arrived at the resort, two days later, Ward had everything arranged. He had me registered in class, had my job all set, and rooms fixed for us to sleep in. Apparently the owners of the resort had traded off timber they had cut from their ski slopes for potatoes. We had them boiled, sliced, fried, French, Dutch, Irish, and plain with butter, with cheese, and with onions. After eleven days of this we tried to introduce these people to a thing called meat. We cooked up some goatburgers for them and finally realized one of the owners' dentures didn't fit and he thought everyone should gum their meals as he did.

We were already three weeks late for the winter semester and the thought of having to catch up in the basket weaving class, not to mention how far I was behind in my life art class was almost too much. This, together with the potato diet and the fact that they didn't have an astrophysics course there at the college, forced us to quit our jobs.

They were having a sorority steak fry the following night so we decided to postpone our quitting until the day after the party. Half way through the steak fry, I mentioned how good the steaks were. The girls were very pleased. They had gotten them real cheap from a truck driver on Route "66". One side, however, had an indentation that looked alot like the bumper of the truck I had seen a few days a before. We backed out of the rest of the party, got all of our gear lashed to the side of the car, and putt-putted away into the night.

Christmas, and we spent it in the living rooms of our respective homes. My parents were especially nice that Christmas. They got my car out of hock for me and I repaid them by being gone for the next five months.

The day after Christmas, Ward and I were standing around in his garage at Manhattan Beach eyeing the surfboards, the skis, and trying to make up our minds what to do, when visions of those lovely girls in ski sweaters began gliding across in front of our eyes.

Ward located a friend of his who was going fishing that afternoon and so with his old .22, a fishing pole, and a sleeping bag, he went aboard the fishing boat bound for Catalina Island. While he was gone for two days, I overhauled the trailer. Actually, all I did was wash off the mud, waxed some skis, and bought some more dry ice to freeze the anticipated goat meat and mackerel, until we could reach the colder climates.

On the 29th of December, while it was still dark outside, we woke up half the neighborhood throwing our equipment into the trailer. The other half woke up when we started north. Our right headlight pointed off to the left and, as we drove by, it hit the houses just about where the second story bedroom windows were located.

First stop on this leg of the trip was Yosemite National Park. There the ski slopes are 23 miles from the lodge.

We flipped to see who got to splint her broken ribs.

The lodge guests are given a meal ticket for lunch so they don't have to drive back and forth. The guests who stay in the hotel are given box lunches, "and such box lunches!". Three sandwiches, chicken, apples, oranges, cookies, and many more nice things. We, of course, arranged our skiing so we could sit at lunch time with a box lunch guest. The leftovers from seven hotel lunches were enough for our lunch and half of our dinner. Boiling the chicken at night, after we had eaten all of the meat off the bones for lunch, took quite awhile to make good soup. Especially at that altitude.

For lift tickets we worked on the ski patrol. Our patrol job didn't last too long. One day the boss caught us flipping a coin to see who got to splint the broken ribs of a buxom movie actress. Twenty-three yards of adhesive tape later, we found out it was her ankle.

We left Yosemite after a week. Fog shrouded the magnificent peaks, as the Buick, trailer in tow, raced by the Ranger's Cabin to save the two dollars park fee. By the time we got down to El Portal, it was raining something fierce. We pulled into a public camp ground, got out, undressed and soaped up our bodies under a tree in the lee of the trailer. About the time we got our bodies soaped and had stepped out into the rain to get showered off, it stopped raining. We climbed somewhat uncomfortably, into our long underwear and sadly drove away.

We bought three gallons of gas in the next station and coasted the rest of the way to Merced. From there, up over Donner Summit and on to Reno. At Mt. Rose we lay in the parking lot for four days. . .too sick to get out of bed and so sick we didn't dare stay in bed. Maybe ptomaine poisoning from the only restaurant meal we had

*I would drive and Ward would ride on the
lee side away from the ducks.*

had in two weeks. . .or maybe the beef was a little too rich for our systems after so much goat meat and mackerel.

In four days we were well enough to travel. We started down off the mountain, dirty, grimey, and moldy, to begin the long trek towards Salt Lake.

In the marshes just west of Winnemucca, Nevada, the ducks were in abundance. We unlimbered our .410 shot gun and .22 caliber rifle. It's a bit tricky to stand on the running board of a car at twentyone below zero at 10 mph, spot a duck, jump off the car, and hit him before he could get out of .410 range (about 45 feet). We traded ninetythree shot gun shells for two ducks and finally got the range. From then on it was easy. I would drive and Ward would ride on the lee side away from the ducks, much the same as the Indians did from their horses when they were attacking covered wagons. I would spot the ducks and he would then fire through the back window of the Buick. We were averaging a duck every second shot when the whole thing went up in flames. Just as Ward pulled the trigger, a truck passed between our car and the duck. With Ward on the lee side of the car, he didn't see the look on the truck driver's face as the shot missed his head by eight inches and took the paint off the top of his truck. Since we were going in opposite directions and the truck couldn't turn around, we felt fairly safe. Besides, we had eighteen ducks already. The legal limit being five, if you have a license, and don't shoot them from a car, and you don't shoot at them with a rifle, and if it is duck season, which it wasn't and we didn't.

ELKO, NEVADA!

We went into the local hotel to use their wash room to

*Ward then crawled under the door of a ten cent toilet
and removed two of the ducks from his coat pockets...*

shave and get cleaned up. With mud up over our knees from breaking through the frozen marches, it was easy to follow our path from the car, thru the lobby to the five cent slot machine, and on to the men's room.

It was nice in the men's room. Steam heat, hot water and the first warm water shave in six days. We mixed up a little of the warm water with some salt and ketchup we brought along and topped off our sponge bath with a hot cup of tomato soup. Ward then crawled under the door of the ten cent toilet and removed two of the ducks from his coat pockets as I stood watch. While I pretended to take a half an hour to shave, he took the same length of time to remove the feathers from the ducks. He was just about through the second one when he decided to flush the feathers down the drain. Apparently, these birds had their winter coats because the feathers jammed up the drain and two pounds of feathers started trickling across the floor headed for the lowest point in the men's room which, in this case, happened to be at the door.

We folded up our gear and Ward stuffed the ducks back into his coat pockets and we sauntered towards the door. I felt a little conspicuous but Ward really looked that way. Especially from behind, as the remaining duck with head intact protruded from a hole in his pocket and every step he took it bounced up and down like a yo-yo.

We were, by this time, fairly clean so we put the ducks back into the trailer and went down the street to spend our ill begotten gambling funds on hot bowls of chili. (We made 40 cents on the nickel machine.)

Driving down the street an hour or so later, headed east for Salt Lake City, I was just starting to unload our guns which we still had in the front seat, when a car be-

*Since we were sitting on the wrong end
of this particular .38 . . .*

hind us honked. We waved it around since our top speed was 34 mph. He honked again. We waved again. By this time, I turned around and watched the car begin to pass us. I leaned over to give forth with some of the dialogue I had learned in the Navy. Just then the window of the car rolled down and an officer of the law sat behind a .38 caliber revolver. Since we were sitting on the wrong end of this particular .38, Ward pulled over and stopped so fast the ski rack broke. The skis kept right on going up the highway. Their actual distance traveled varied with their individual wax job.

They parked on an angle in front of us so we couldn't get away while they were walking to the car. I began to wonder what we had done. One sheriff came around to my side of the car, with revolver drawn, while the other stood four feet away from Ward's side and said: "Let's see your driver's license."

"I don't have one", Ward said. It had actually expired four years ago.

"Where is the registration for your license plates?"

"I just sent it in for new ones", I lied. Actually, I had left it in the men's room with a map of Elko, on which I had made a notation of the bank's location, when we made our get-away after the feather flushing incident.

"Where are your new license tabs?"

"We didn't get them in the mail yet."

"Are those guns loaded?"

"Yes."

"Why?"

"In case we get held up."

Tactician that he was, Ward came forth: "If you fellows are going to be so belligerent why don't you take us to jail?"

They did!

We got truly warm for the first time since Christmas. Bars or no bars, this place really had it. We sat for half an hour on the two steam heaters in the lobby of the jail. As the heat began to creep through our clothes and into our bodies, the odor of the mackerel and goat meat we had been sleeping with for several weeks began to be unleashed. Like a tidal wave of previous arrests, I could see it was turning the law enforcement officers against us with each passing moment.

The booking sergeant finally came back from his afternoon game of pool and had a good heart-to-heart talk with us. I could have understood him better if he only would have stopped squirting that airwick at us with every other word. He went on hissing and snorting like a leaky valve. I must admit we were a lot more acceptable after our interview. We had been picked up because someone matching our descriptions had stolen a car like mine in Reno. We identified ourselves conclusively by telling them what was in the bottom of our sleeping bags. Goat meat, dry ice, mackerel, and chickens. Old chickens.

"Where did all of the duck feathers come from?"

"Down sleeping bags."

"Make them out of mallards now?"

"Army surplus, you know."

We got out of town as fast as what money we had left would let us. In our confusion we somehow headed in the wrong direction. As darkness began to fall we boiled back into Winnemucca. Still couldn't afford Anti-Freeze. We parked under the lights of a neon motel sign and began to cook dinner. The blinking of the sign made me feel as though I had hiccups of the eyeballs. We decided to save the ducks for a time when we could really use a change of diet. They were frozen solid by this time anyway and would stay that way in our ice box trailer.

Dinner was the usual bowl of soup, a goat meat chop or two and a half dozen cups of tea each. The last two or three cups were more like sugared water since one tea bag will only go so far.

We motored around a bit after dinner in search of a place to park the car and sleep. A sudden windstorm had come up and plummeted the thermometer to 37 degrees below zero. We finally found a nice white barn to sleep behind. After our usual routine of emptying the sleeping bags of goat meat and mackerel, compounded by the addition of 18 ducks, we climbed into bed. About midnight the storm center passed over and instead of being in the lee of the barn we were on the windward side. The rest of the night we were buffeted about like a boat in a hurricane.

As the first grey streaks of dawn began to creep through our ice encrusted windows, I was awakened by the roar of an airplane over head. About the same time I was lifted right out of my bed when it missed the top of our trailer by eight feet. The prop blast almost tipped the trailer over. Instantly I was out in the snow in my mummy

. . . like a gunnysack on a pogo stick.

bag, hopping around like a gunny sack on a pogo stick. My eyes began to focus on the white barn. We were parked alongside the main hangar of the Winnemucca airport. As a matter of fact, we were right in the middle of the landing strip. The pilot buzzed again and dropped a wrench that punched a hole in one side of the trailer, with a note explaining politely to "get the car the hell off the landing strip 'cuz I don't have enough gas to circle once more." We tried to move it but the car was too frozen to the ground by wind driven snow. By the time we got moving, the radiator was boiling. So we put a pan of snow on the radiator to melt for coffee. The plane sputtered twice and began its long, silent glide toward total destruction against the side of our trailer. We ran for cover just as the plane set down so hard it bounced clear over the trailer and slid to a stop in a snow bank about 300 yards up the runway. The pilot stumbled out of the plane and lumbered towards our trailer. Suddenly he reached the end of the extension cord on his flying suit and lit up like a Christmas tree when a short circuit occurred. Meantime, our coffee water got hot. Ward unzipped me from my mummy bag so I could help him push, and we boiled away once again headed east towards who knows what.

Plagued by a constant blizzard, we moved rather slowly across the rest of Nevada and into Utah. East, ever farther, into a land made famous by gunfighters and Indians and television screens, and now slowly being desecrated as we plowed through the snow drifts.

By late afternmoon, one of the windshield wipers dangled like wet spaghetti from the bracket and the other cleared a spot only big enough to peek through. That is, if you didn't mind peeking straight up in the air. Ward

My eyes began to focus on the white barn.

was once again taking his turn at the wheel when we were overtaken by a hard riding cowboy. He swerved his ice covered horse in front of us just as we rounded a bend. There, in the road ahead, was his herd of 347 razorback hogs. They looked like white moles in a bowl of rice. Caught out in the south 10,000 acres of the Lazy Bar S by the fast moving storm, they were having quite a time as the new snow came clear up over their heads. Ward somehow managed to get the car stopped before he ran over the herd and the cowboy. A bit of frontier type of palaver, sly inuendos about our nice, warm, heated car, and his rapidly dwindling herd when Ward suggested: "Why not let us go ahead in the car? The hogs could then wallow single file along behind us in the tracks the car makes in the deep powder snow".

One hour later, we were driving down the main street of Wells, Nevada, followed by the hogs and a hungry cowboy. When we finally got inside the restaurant, it was plain to see (smell) how long the cowboy had been taking care of hogs. I felt as uncomfortable as the people sitting next to me in the theater in Las Vegas must have felt.

Three days later, I read in the Salt Lake paper that a rotary snowplow had chewed up 223 hogs when the hogs mistook the plow's squeaking axles for a hog caller.

After dinner and sad goodbyes, we were clanking our way across the salt marshes to the west of Salt Lake City, when the holes in the radiator got bigger and belched out their last remaining bit of H_2O. As we boiled into Salt Lake City we were a sorry sight indeed. The bottom of the car was a foot thick with ice. Steam out of the radiator had frozen over the windshield. To pilot the car, Ward stood on the running board and steered with his right hand while I sat in the driver's seat and applied brakes, clutch, and gas, as he would call for them. After an hour of groping, a garage was located that would let us in to fix the radiator. I went next door to the grocery store to get some rice to put in the radiator to glue up the leaks. All I could get was tapioca pudding. While we cooked some for the radiator and a side dish for the gas station attendant, we used his phone to call one of Ward's friends. Turned out his friend was now the owner of a string of house trailers. He had parlayed these house trailers into a beautiful house overlooking the city with maids and butlers and things. The trailers? Oh, he used them to tour the W.A.C. camps during the war. Ran a string of "he" whorehouses.

Ward's friend was nice enough to offer us the sanctuary of his home where we could rid ourselves of the grime and dirt of the eight-day trip from Reno. When he met us at the door he was very nice but very insistent that we enter his house through the bathroom window. After washing up, taking a bath, then a shower and then shaving, I felt much better and four pounds lighter. We sat around the living room talking and soaking up some of his heat and finally fell asleep on the floor. The rug was the softest I have ever slept on, especially after sleeping in the trailer on a frozen mattress for a month.

During the night the police came twice and tried to haul our car and trailer away. Claimed they had received four phone calls about a wreck in the neighborhood. They couldn't get the car out of gear. This and the fact that the horn honked every time they opened the door made the whole thing practically burglar proof. Not being a very good electrician I had fixed the horn one day after it fell off at a stop sign. Now it would honk every time you put the brakes on. This wasn't too bad, but the headlights would go off every time we turned left. This wasn't too much of a problem in the city, but in the mountains it was almost disastrous. We solved it by holding onto a flashlight and turning it on every time a left turn loomed ahead. After assuring the policemen we would move the wreck in the morning, we curled up on that soft rug right next to the floor furnace. We had been cold for so long that the heater really felt good. About 3:45 A.M. I awoke to the smell of burning feathers. Ward had rolled onto the floor furnace and fired up the foot of his mummy bag. I managed to get mine unzipped and groped for the door. By then Ward had hopped through the pall of smoke into the bathroom and there he sat on the edge of the toilet, cooling off his burning feet in the only instantly available source of deep water in the house. The rest of the night was more or less uneventful except for two or three more interruptions from phone calls from men looking for work in the house trailers.

The sunshine the next day warmed up the air to about nineteen below zero so we had our usual radiator thaw out trouble.

We now had it down to a pretty good science. To thaw it out we would take a long stick, wrap it in old rags and soak the rags in gasoline. Then we would start the car. Once the car was running, we would light the rags, then with the flames about eight feet high we would hold this in front of the radiator. The fan from the engine would suck the flames through the radiator and theoretically thaw out the ice. The only problem was the amount of gasoline to use. The third time we tried this I put too much gasoline on the rag and it not only thawed out the ice but melted the distributor cap, burned the wire off

. . .cooling off his burning feet in the only instantly available source of deep water in the house.

the plugs and thawed out the inside of the car for the first time in three months.

With Alta about 20 miles from Salt Lake City we drove it in about four and a half hours. This, of course, is with time off for the dinner we had in the suburbs. Nice light overhead (hooked onto a telephone pole), the stove was working well and we really enjoyed our sauerkraut and weiners. Washed it down with a couple of cups of hot tea (same old bag). We were sitting on the curb drinking the cups of tea, with the smell of sauerkraut everywhere, when our old friends the cops showed up. They were at first suspicious of the hot tea and accused us of being drunk. Why else would anyone sit on a curb, leaning against a snowbank, in the middle of winter eating dinner? We filled their sobriety balloons with sauerkraut gas, which I know the sergeant is still trying to figure out.

Next morning we were once again saying hello to our old friends at Alta. It was clear, cold, and the skiing was fantastic. New powder, but the same old lift prices. We climbed all day long and that night got our jobs back again, cooking hamburgers, at the Snow Pine Lodge. Our jobs didn't start until the weekend so, that night, we decided to have a roast duck dinner. We rigged the tarp behind the trailer, lit the lantern and started things off by trying to cut up the duck. It was frozen harder than the pot we were going to cook it in. We finally squeezed it into little pieces by putting it between the jack and an axle of the car and then trying to jack up the car. We had duck Stroganoff, of a type. Sometimes referred to as pressed duck . . . and this one was really flat. Tasted nice with leftover tapioca on the side. This was also frozen and tasted a bit like wild rice. Almost like the buckshot left in the duck. It wasn't until we got to the bottom of the pot

We filled their sobriety balloons with sauerkraut gas.

that Ward found the glove I had been using to work the jack.

Ten days of this freezing and skiing and we were ready for warmer things. One cold afternoon we met two girls who had just returned from Sun Valley. They talked at length of the HOT water swimming pools and the ski runs and the nice restaurants and the free busses and the good food. After the mention of free hot water swimming pools, our ears really perked up. Imagine, soaking in that hot water till it invaded your bones. A body that hadn't been warm for a month or so. "Say, we might even be able to bring along a bar of soap and kill two birds with one towel." Of course, we would have to be careful since we didn't want to use the wrong kind of soap. Might leave a ring around the swimming pool.

Once again we piled our junk into the trailer and left the parking lot headed down to Salt Lake City. Things were going along fairly well. Car, very slow, only one headlight, people honking at us to get out of the way, headlight not working on left turns. Ward was trying to pick up something on our radio, which only worked if you were within twenty miles of a station. Bent over the steering wheel I was concious of a very definite lurch. Looking out the window, I saw a wheel roll by the car and leap over the snowbank alongside the road to disappear in the darkness. There we sat. In the middle of the road with only five wheels where six were needed. The left trailer wheel was missing, out of sight down the canyon. The canyon, at this point, seemed to be bottomless. We located a dime in an old pair of levis, flipped it, I lost and had to go in search of the wheel. Walking down a hill like that in daylight is difficult . . . at night, it was impossible. Very steep and with powder snow up to my armpits, the flashlight on my crash helmet, I followed the marks the tire had left whenever it hit a high spot in the snow.

At the bottom of the canyon, I finally located it in a stream that was frozen over for all of its thirty miles of length except for fifty feet on either side of where the tire sank. As soon as I wrestled it out of the water it froze instantly and I felt a like hog mover in a deep freeze plant. How do you carry a twenty five pound tire, covered with sixty pounds of ice, up a forty five degree slope in snow up to your armpits? I hollered to Ward and he threw down a rope. This I tied around the tire and then hand over hand, I wallowed back to the car.

I lay exhausted in the road as Ward hauled the tire back up to the trailer.

We still had no anti-freeze in the car. We couldn't run the motor without water. The car heater wouldn't work without the motor running so to get warm, we filled a can with gasoline and lit it. By the light of the twelve foot high flames we managed to warm up enough to get the wheel back on the trailer and drive away just as the fire department drove up.

That night in Salt Lake City, we slept in the back yard of our only remaining friend. In the early morning hours, we snuck into his bathroom, took hot showers and sped north at 25 mph through Ogden, Twin Falls, Shoshone. Here we unlimbered our guns once again. Tramping through the twenty-four inches of snow that covered the plains around Shoshone, we saw rabbit tracks by the thousands. Ward used the shotgun and I banged away with the .22. He would get a shotgun shot while they were running. When they stopped, I would get a rifle shot at them. By the time we shot eleven of them, the ten below zero weather had frozen most of the ones we were carrying around. The only water we could find to clean them in was the local irrigation ditch. It took some ten minutes of chopping to get through the eleven inches of ice. The water we exposed would then freeze instantly. We chopped the rabbits up like kindling.

At dusk, easing, (rather, I should say sneaking) into the parking lot at Sun Valley, was our outfit. We found a place in one corner where we would be somewhat inconspicuous and there lit our lantern, stove, and cooked our first meal in this, the world's greatest ski resort, Sun Valley, Idaho.

Dinner over, we started to look around and much to our pleasure we spotted the hot water swimming pools and found showers down the halls for some of the guests who couldn't afford them in their rooms. We assumed these showers could also be used by people who couldn't afford rooms. Next day we looked for a job but not too hard. After figuring out how to get on the lift, we skied all afternoon. How we sneaked on, without paying, will go to our graves with us. Our methods were so good that, years afterwards, when the number of people sneaking on the lift got out of hand, Sun Valley management called me in to help them redesign their lift tickets, so sneaking on has now become much more difficult. (Of course, I didn't tell them all my secrets!)

Day after day, after day, we would get on the lift at 8:00 in the morning and ski almost non-stop until the lift shut down for the night. Our rabbits lasted almost two weeks, then another trip to Shoshone, another batch of rabbits. During the winter we had rabbits fixed almost every way you can imagine. . . fried, boiled, singed, burnt. We

Lunch was the big problem.

even ate them like a popsicle.

Lunch was actually the only big problem. On the tables of all the restaurants at that time were bowls of oyster crackers for soup buying patrons. We found if you take an oyster cracker and dip it in a bit of ketchup it is fairly edible. If you dip enough of them, they have a tendency to make you think you have had enough to eat. Of course, this involves a couple of full bowls of crackers since they're mostly air. Sort of like opening your mouth and running into the wind. Occasionally, you can have a dab of mustard on them for variety. On cold, snowy days, cold oyster crackers and ketchup don't warm you up very much. We would take a paper cup from the drinking fountain and go back and ask the lady for "some more hot water for our tea bag?" Take it back to the table, squirt some ketchup into it for flavor, add some oyster crackers for body, some salt and pepper, and have a fairly edible bowl of tomato soup. Once in a while we broke down and had a candy bar. I recall one afternoon when we watched someone drinking hot tea by the cup full. It looked so good we invested ten cents in a cup of tea. The combination of minerals, the altitude, the tea, the scalding water (boiled under pressure) all put together we managed to stretch our tea bag through eleven cups of hot water. That night we stopped at the grocery store and bought forty-eight bags of tea for fifty cents and from then on had tea at the rate of one cent for eleven cups. . .or .0091 cents a cup.

We skied hard every day and our skiing managed to improve a bit until we finally decided to enter a race for the guests. By this time, all of the guests thought we were employees and all of the employees thought we were guests. A very convenient sort of an arrangement because

I took the first gate like Grant took Richmond.

WARREN MILLER '57

. . .and on the fifth gate I flopped . . .

. . . at six below zero we got out Ward's ice cream freezer.

we got employees' discounts together with guest privileges. I could tell you how we learned to ski, stem this, stem that, rotate this, lean this way, that way, but all of this sort of technique thing is a subject unto itself. Actually, we eavesdropped on the ski school classes. The only injury I had all winter was in this race I just mentioned. I shoved out of the starting gate, took the third gate like Grant took Richmond and on the fifth gate, I flopped, sustaining a sprained right thumb that kept me off of skis for three days. (I couldn't hold my thumb over the expired date on my lift ticket.)

Each winter at Sun Valley, they have a race or two, or three, which draws a big name field. One of these, at the time, called The President's Cup, was a three way combined. Downhill, slalom, and jumping. The jumping tournament was held over on Ruud Mt. Sitting in the car with Ward and two girl friends watching the men jump we got a little bored after awhile. With the thermometer at six below zero, we got out Ward's ice cream freezer that we just happened to bring along, threw in the ingredients and when the men weren't hurtling through the air we took turns getting warm by turning the handle on the freezer. By the time the tournament was over, we had a gallon of ice cream which we took downtown and swapped for four hamburger steak dinners.

When we parked the trailer in the corner of the parking lot, we had only planned on staying a week or two, so we just kicked a hole in the snow to put our garbage in. When the hole filled up, we stomped another hole alongside the first one and filled it. Fifteen days and nine holes later, I was asleep one morning when the hotel detectives came around and asked us to move our camp so they could have the parking lot plowed out. We couldn't get

*We couldn't even get the car
started, much less move it.*

Undressing, we broke the ice, and plunged in . . .

the car started, much less move it. They finally brought a tractor to move us, since our wheels were frozen to the ground. An hour later we stood 100 feet from the original parking place, cooking breakfast. The rotary snowplow came roaring through our campground spraying snow, milk cartons, old rabbit carcases, bread wrappers, tin cans, and pink paper napkins all over the trees behind our camp site. They had hit our garbage pit. From then on, whenever anyone wanted to find our place, we just told them to go to the parking lot and look for the tree with the rabbits hanging from the top. We would be right under it. Only tree I've ever seen that could grow both canned orange juice and milk cartons at the same time.

Again, a rabbit hunting trip south to Shoshone. We were stumbling around through the snow when we raised a few ducks that were wintering in a farmer's feed lot. Without a moments hesitation, we opened up with the shotgun and the .22. One duck spiraled down and we broke into a run to grab it as it hit the ground. Instead, it went into a long glide just before it hit and coasted to the other side of the river. It was a nice, warm, winter afternoon, lots of sun, some snow underfoot and all that seperated us from a duck dinner was 60 feet of swiftly flowing ice water. Undressing, we broke the ice, plunged in and swam across. Floundering out on the other side I had such a headache from the cold water I was blind. Neither of us saw the duck swimming back across the river to where we had just left. We then proceeded, naked as two jaybirds, to run up and down the bank on the far side, in a vain effort to get the blood to flow again, completely forgetting the duck.

"Can I help you?", a VERY feminine voice startled both of us into a long, low, flat dive back into the icy water. There we sat immersed in this swift-flowing deep freeze, up to our chins in mud, water frozen in our hair, teeth chattering so much we couldn't answer. I finally managed to stutter out:

"My friend fell in and I dove in to save him. Would you run for help?" Instead of running she reloaded and fired the guns we had left on the bank and started screaming like a banshee. Before we knew it seventeen children showed up from nowhere. She and her science class from the local high school were on a field trip looking for minerals in the lava formations. With the group more or less evenly divided between boys and girls we felt a little out of it since we forgot to bring our clothes. By now we were encased in so much ice we wouldn't have been embarrassed to climb out of the water in front of anyone. We were swimming back across the river to retrieve our clothes when I realized the only things we had to dry off with were waterproof nylon parkas, scratchy wool ski pants, and our underwear. We donned it all and felt our underwear soak up the water like a sponge, only to freeze once again when it oozed through to the outside.

The hunting trip was somewhat of a success, however, since the school teacher invited us over to her house to warm up, meet her folks and cook some of our rabbits on her stove. In all this confusion the duck we had shot managed to rearrange the two feathers Ward hit and swam off downstream out of gunshot range. There he once again became airborne to go south where the swimming is a little warmer.

Now love walked into my life in the form of a gorgeous girl with a southern accent as thick as the Mason-Dixon Line. She couldn't tell one end of the ski from the other, but she was lovely and danced like a dream. Operator that I am, I bought two employee's tickets to the Opera House, managed to sneak by the ticket taker and still have the tickets left so I could get a refund and buy her a beer later on. Next day, I showed her how to do a kick turn and she let me eat the potato chips from the hamburger she bought. It was love. . . four dates later I found out she had a $28.00 a day room in the Lodge. I thought our romance was over. Little did I realize it was just starting. Walks to Ketchum; ten cent beers; more movies snuck into; we even went bowling. She bowled. I set the pins. Then one morning she said: "I have to go into Hailey to catch a plane. Will you drive me down?" With no regular airlines serving Hailey I thought this a bit strange but said: "Sure". Next morning I dug the car out and tried to get it started. Impossible. Two feet of ice and snow were covering the whole thing. It was a bitter cold day at ten below zero. I got a truck to push us up and down the parking lot a few times but the Buick wouldn't start. Then he pushed us up onto the highway. With just a patch of snow cleared away from the window, visibility was at a minimum. I could see straight ahead. As we were getting pushed towards Ketchum, it still wouldn't start. We got pushed faster, ten, fifteen, twenty, thirty, forty mph almost to Ketchum. Now we were going over eighty mph and I still couldn't hear the motor running. I got a little panicky and told my girl friend to stick her head out of the door and tell the guy pushing us to slow down a bit 'cuz we were getting close to town. She stuck her head out but there was no one there. Our own motor was running, the throttle was stuck wide open and all of the snow on the car had insulated the motor so well we couldn't hear it. We roared down the main street at eightyfive mph with the horn on full blast, I was bent over trying desperately to unjam the throttle, or the clutch at least, which was also frozen. By the time we got things unstuck we had run off the road, through a plowed field and were two hundred yards from the highway. Fortunately, the ground was frozen hard and the wheels just fit into the plowed furrows.

With all of this mixup, I thought my girl friend would miss her plane, but enroute she told me it would wait since it was her own. A nice comfortable DC3. I slowly put two and two together, had some conversation with the pilot and copilot and discovered her father was one of the deep south's richest men. And that included Texas. And I snuck her into a movie. . . least she could have done was offer to buy the beer afterwards. It took hours to get all of the trunks and gear out of the tired Buick and onto the plane. By then the below zero temperature had again crept back into the engine. I waved goodbye to my love and her DC3 and then tried to start the engine. It was frozen tighter than a bung in a 1933 vintage wine barrel. I had spent what little money I had entertaining the Southern belle so a tow truck was out of the question. The small airport had shut down when the DC3 took off. With no one around the landing strip or hangers, town four miles away, and my sleeping bags another ten miles from there, in an equally below zero trailer, I thought back to the canyon in Alta when we got warm by a gasoline fire.

Grubbing around I found the same gasoline can with the holes in the side of it under a four week old pile of dirty clothes, eleven stiff rabbits and two quarts of milk that had been frozen for so long they no longer had a carton around them. (We ate pieces of milk like popsicles). At any rate, I now had the can and the next problem was to get some gasoline into it, control the heighth of the flames, place the blazing can on the ground under the motor and let the heat creep up into the oil, thus warming it up enough to have the tired battery turn the engine over. Two problems existed. 1. How to control the flames? 2. How to get the gas out of the car and into the can? I had no hose to siphon it with so I dug out a pair of pliers and wrestled the plug out of the bottom of the gas tank and drained some gas into the can. The gas was the same temperature as the air, 23 below zero, so when I tried to put the plug back into the car the gas dribbled down my arm as far as my shoulder, gradually filling up my armpit. I couldn't do anything till I got the plug back in. My right arm was getting ready to sell to Birdseye Frozen Foods when I finally managed to wiggle the plug back in the car. A match, a mild explosion. I wiped the soot from my eyes and tried to control the height of the flames so they wouldn't come through the top of the hood. By the time I figured this out, all of the gas had burned out of the can. Only place left to get gas now was from and ancient crop dusting plane that was leaning against the hanger.

The gas must have been mixed with equal parts of insecticide and old grasshoppers. It smelled like low tide in a marsh flat, but made an awe inspiring flame. I shoved the can under the car and just as I was congratulating myself on how well things were going I noticed flames coming out of the front seat of the car. The flames were so big, I couldn't reach under the car and drag the can out. The starter wouldn't work, so I ran around behind and started pushing. The tires were frozen to the ground. I managed to slide the car about eight feet but the car was fifteen feet long. When the can finally ran out of gas, and the flames dies out the back seat was warm enough to sit in. The only trouble was the engine wasn't in the back seat.

The starter wouldn't work, so I ran around behind
and started pushing.

Time flies in a resort like Sun Valley and between wealthy Southern girls and skiing and skiing and wealthy Southern girls, the season was running out.

One night while in a bistro with the unlikely name of The Casino, I was sitting with the boys enjoying a game of four handed Acey Ducey. We were talking about our service records and this guy had this medal and this one had that medal and I couldn't brag about anything I had done in the war except having been sunk in a hurricane.

After we were rescued from our ship wreck, we spent a month or so on Guadalcanal. With the war having long ago left this part of the Pacific there was not much to do except try and figure out how much time we could spend doing nothing at all. This was split up between trading the natives T-shirts for sea shells and trading sea shells to sailors on transient ships for milk. We were back in the bush one day and saw how the natives neglected their children when the idea struck me!

"Let's trade some old clothes for one of these children." Then we'll raise the child with the pet dogs on the ship. Treat it like a human being, but never speak in front of it. The only conversation the baby would ever hear would be dog talk. The baby would then learn how to talk with dogs and at the age of nine or ten we would then teach him how to speak English. Send him to high school, college, and then Veterinarian school. Our baby would then know how to talk "dog talk" and when people brought their dogs in to him he could ask them what was wrong by barking with them. With his bark, our drumming up customers and his diagnosis, we would then make a million dollars by very little work. American Free Enterprise.

The snow was 400 feet deep and moving horizontally at 83 mph.

The following morning, I was coming back from shaving in the lodge when the low, scudding clouds had once again built up into a full scale Idaho type blizzard. Which means the snow is four hundred feet deep and moving horizontally at about 83 mph. The high wind had tipped over the trailer and trapped Ward inside. It was so covered with snow that no one noticed it. I dug Ward out and we moved to leeward of the parking lot and began to gather our socks, underwear, Rice Krispies, and long johns from off the side of The Skier's Chalet. There were others caught in the high wind, too. When we sorted out the clothes at the end of the storm, we had an extra boot, three extra gloves, and a pair of tickets to "Oklahoma" for the following night in San Diego. I never could explain the set of false teeth we found.

One blizzard on top of another finally began to wear the edge off skiing, so Ward got a job. Real, honest to goodness work. He is a very good photographer so they employed him in the dark room developing and printing the pictures they take around the Valley every day. He reported for work at sundown and spent the night agitating trays of hypo and cropping low camera angle shots of movie stars so they would look as if they were schussing Exhibition. Then when the sun began to appear again he would stumble out of the darkroom into the bright light and new snow. After about fifteen days of working all night and skiing all day he began making round trips on the lift. The money was good but during lunch hour one day we held a board of directors meeting. It was "say goodbye to the job," or quit skiing. We decided he could work in the summer and since he was there to ski, he phoned up the lab and quit. Gone were the paychecks every two weeks, gone was the wonderful food in the employee's cafeteria. Back to frozen milk, frozen Rice

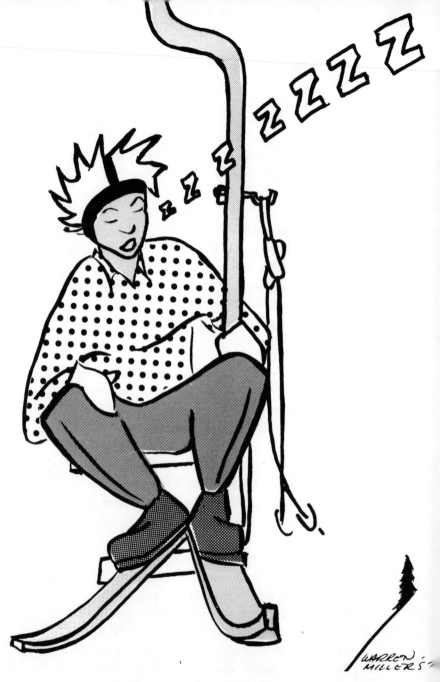

. . .he began making round trips on the lift.

Crispies, frozen fingers, and sneaking on the lift once again.

We began to get a little tired of oyster crackers and ketchup and brought along all kinds of goodies. Smoked herring, kippered herring, hardboiled eggs, pickles, potato chips. We brought them in a rucksack and one day got set for a big feast. Small problem. We had deposited the rucksack on a table in the Roundhouse while we skied. Our hard boiled eggs, we found, had never been cooked. Merely frozen. The warm room thawed them, thawed the herring and the mackerel and through a small hole in the bottom of the rucksack this unlikely lunch was slowly spreading its' deathly look across the table when the manager smelled it. He threw the whole mess (and us) out in the snow. It would have been OK but our cameras were in the same rucksack. I tried to explain what happened to the insurance man but he just laughed and said: "prove it". I couldn't. No one would believe my story.

Which brings up a rather important point. In the last forty years I have told many of the stories you are reading. Very few people believe them when I tell them in person. When I begin to read them in print, I find it difficult to believe them myself. There were, however, many people at Sun Valley at the time this happened. People of influence and good judgement. Successful businessmen who didn't believe it when it was actually happening. They would, however, I am sure, if you could contact them, vouch for every story you read herein. If you are in any doubt of their authenticity, send me a stamped, self-addressed, ten dollar bill and I will be happy to phone you and talk a bit about the old days when it was really cold; when we were skiing at Sun Valley, Idaho

Another Warren Miller Production available in pool halls everywhere or consult your local police officer for further details.

for eighteen cents a day, all inclusive.

About two miles from the lodge is a place called Trail Creek Cabin. This is an evening spa and those with money enough, hire a sleigh and horses, ride up, have dinner, dance and return in the sleigh for $2.50. Our ambition was to go to this place some evening and try some of the fried chicken we had been hearing about for most of the winter. Finally, the opportunity came when we were invited by some old, old friends from Los Angeles. Turned out later they thought we were paying for it and we knew they would HAVE to pay for it. After we were invited, I got my suit out of the duffle bag where it had been wrinkling most of the winter and tried it on. It looked awful. I borrowed an iron and flattened it out. Now the creases in the pants were on the sides instead of at random. We met our dates in the lobby of the Inn, went out, climbed into the sleigh, and bounced up to Trail Creek. Might as well not have pressed the suit. The two mile ride in a hay rack with horse blankets, girls, and wine bottles rolling around made the suit look like I had just slept in it. Actually, I DID when it was real cold. The party was nice and, between the four of us, we consumed 43 chicken legs, eighteen wings, nine glasses of milk, seven desserts, and two cups of coffee. Ward and I didn't drink coffee. Keeps you awake. Fortunately, I had put waxed paper in the pockets of my overcoat so the chicken helpings I snuck into them didn't stain the coat. Tasted nice for the next five days.

We finally boiled the last bowl of soup out of the bones a week or so later. As a matter of fact, we had it the same night the girls left for Los Angeles.

One thing I have never mentioned is the problem of

It takes an acrobat . . .

going to bed, after a date, dressed in overcoat, white shirt, and suit, and dancing type shoes. It takes an acrobat to stand outside in the below zero weather, undo your shoe laces, then your belt and pants, rebutton the top button, then undo your tie, shirt coat, and overcoat, slip out of all three of your garments at the same time, hang them on a hanger and hope the wind doesn't blow them away during the night. Once out of these you then sit on the edge of the bed, your fanny is now inside the trailer, pull off your pants and shoes at the same time, stand on the ice by the trailer in your stocking feet, (it melts if you stand on it longer than 23 seconds), hang up your pants, slip your shoes under the trailer out of the way, and climb into a frozen bed. By this time you are so wide awake you lay staring at the ceiling for the next hour and a half while you warm up the sleeping bag. Next morning, three inches of new powder is in your pants pockets and the powder on the shoulders of your suit hanging outside on the hanger, looks like dandruff in a hair tonic ad.

One day blended into the next, with a mad dash of skis, powder snow, ice, girls, movies, skis, and then one morning we awoke to hear the pitter patter of rain on the roof. I rolled over and looked out the open door into a pool of mud. What was once beautiful snow around the trailer was now a quagmire of potato peelings, milk cartons, banana peels, and some bits of thawed out rabbit. I felt a little uncomfortable with the water up around the bottom of our beds and I felt a little lost as I watched my ski boots sail down wind towards the far side of this gigantic puddle. Fortunately, they were waterproof and didn't sink but ran aground about a hundred feet away.

This sudden spring thaw made us get off the dime and

. . .with a mad dash of skis, powder snow, girls, ice, girls. . .

out of the water and decide it was now time to go some-where else for spring skiing. We knew we should go home but since the employees had been so nice to us all winter long, we decided to give them a party.

First, we moved the trailer to higher ground. Next a trip to Shoshone for rabbits. By this time we had become expert shots and by nightfall, there were seventythree rabbits in the car. Seventytwo of which had been shot and one I ran over on the way home. When we got back to Sun Valley, it was almost midnight. With seventythree rabbits to clean (at midnight) there were only two places available. One was the Big Wood River, which, of course, was very cold at this time of the night. The other place was the showers of The Skier's Chalet. Common sense will dictate where we did it. With Ward skinning the rabbits and me doing the rest, we had rabbits in the showers, on the floor, in the wash basin . . .we had them everywhere. We had blood up to our elbows, when into this mess staggered a drunken guest just back from Ketchum. He wanted to take a shower. He couldn't even get in the door. Since he was paying good money for his accomodations, he thought this sort of thing deserved a complaint to the management. By the time he went through the proper channels and got the hotel detective out of bed to throw us out, we had cleaned up the mess and spirited our rabbits and ourselves back to the deep freeze of our trailer. When the police finally arrived they found no rabbits, no mess. All they found was some blood and a hair in a corner of one of the showers. They thought the drunk was lying and instead that someone had been done in.

Four hours later a very sober guest was pointing an accusing finger at the police through jail bars and finally

We moved the trailer to higher ground.

WARREN MILLER '57

We had seventy rabbits to clean in the wash basins.

convinced them he was telling the truth. In the meantime, they had staged a full scale murder investigation: all of the guests rooms had been checked, employees checked, and the only people that were missing was a couple who were last seen checking into a motel on the outskirts of town.

The next morning, we had managed to swipe half a cord of wood from a restaurant downtown. A friend had gotten four cases of cokes from some mysterious source, potato chips from someone else, lettuce and the makings of a salad from another place and, by three in the afternoon, the 73 rabbits began to cook at an alarmingly slow rate on the two burner stove. By seven, we were hosting the biggest party the parking lot had ever seen . . . thirty-eight guests. With a well cooked?? rabbit dinner for everyone, salad and the works. We had quite an evening. Music was supplied by Ward's girl friend who played the accordian in the Roundhouse. All who attended pronounced it the best party of the season. About one-thirty with the bonfire slowly dying and the people full of rabbit, song, and good cheer, we sat down together, Ward and I, and decided that we should be leaving Sun Valley very soon. Preferably, very early the next morning.

We wanted to complete our visit to every ski resort west of Denver . . . Jackson Hole, Aspen, Alta, and then home. We had no money left but we had a car and the desire for the trip. As luck would have it, at the party we met two people who wanted to take a similar trip. They had some money but no car. We teamed up. And so these "two waitresses" and Ward and I set off early the next morning for Jackson Hole, Wyoming.

Enroute to Jackson Hole, you drive through Craters of

*By three o'clock preparations began to get under way
for our party.*

the Moon, where we stopped off for some hunting. This time I hit a wild feathered thing of some sort to add to our food supply. Again, the problem of cleaning it.

A tank full of gas in Arco, Idaho. While it was being filled, Ward went into the men's room. A half hour later, when he came out, I had checked all four tires three times, filled the radiator, checked the stove, and tightened the license plate. He looked silly with the plucked bird under his arm. That's probably the only men's room in the state of Idaho that boasts a feather lined waste basket.

At this time, sugar rationing was still on and we had run out of stamps. Having used the same tea bag for the last nineteen cups, it took a lot of sugar to make it taste good. We decided that without ration stamps, the only way we could get some more sugar would be to go into a restaurant and order some ice cream. At least one of the four of us would be able, at one time or another, to steal a sugar container from the counter. After making a check out list of how we would get the waitress out to the kitchen as often as possible, we walked in. Forty-five minutes later, when we were half a mile up the road, I pulled a sugar bowl out of my pocket, "this should last us at least a week." Three other people said in chorus, "I didn't think you got one so I stole one, too!"

In Victor, Wyoming, we ran out of milk. Visiting all the stores in town, we found out that it was too early in the year to buy milk. Seems as though everyone in town had their own cows. We finally talked the shoemaker into selling us a couple of quarts of his morning squeezings. The only thing we had to put in was a collapsible bucket, which later that day, it DID. All over the trailer.

*By seven we were hosting the biggest party
the parking lot had ever seen.*

It had feathers, flew and tasted awful.

From Victor on over Teton Pass. It was March, almost April, now and the road was clear and dry. We drove by a "Chains Required" sign like it wasn't even there and started around a corner and up the hill for the pass. We got as far as our momentum would let us and then the smoothe tires wouldn't bite into the glass ice on the shady side of the road. I swung over to the sunny side and almost ran off the road but hit a snow bank that kept us from pitching through space. The trailer skidded into the bank, teetered crazily, the door swung open and threw half of our surplus gear out on the highway. The gals went back and retrieved their skivvies which had popped out of one of the suitcases that flew open. Ward gathered up our long johns and things while I put on the chains. Each chore took about as long as the other and an hour later, we ground our way up and over another a pass.

In the frontier town of Jackson Hole, spring had really sprung. Hot, slushy snow. A few sleepy cowboys waiting for the arrival of the first summer tourist. The gambling halls had a couple of "Gunsmoke " type characters betting money that there were more flies in the window than people in town. We couldn't wait for the final tally but went on over to the lift.

It was closed . . . season over.

SOUTHEAST NOW TOWARDS DENVER

There are portions of this road that are so desolate it is difficult to imagine that you are in the U.S. In spots, the road stretched farther than the eye could see in either direction. I was driving along at about 55 mph downhill when the engine sighed to a stop. Sounded exactly as though it was out of gas. We checked and found we still had a gallon and a half. After two hours of searching,

On the third step I was running in my stocking feet.

Ward discovered that the distributor points had broken. The engine couldn't fire and there we were. In the two hours it took to find the trouble, only one car had gone by and it was going in the wrong direction. We grubbed through our tools, spare parts, wax kits, bottom of sleeping bags, and finally in one of the girl's jewelry boxes we ran across a set of points for a '33 Plymouth. The fact that they would work in a 1937 Buick was amazing. Ward, mechanical genius that he is, made them work with a pair of pliers and a file and we used them for the balance of the trip.

Along about dusk we were looking for a place to stop and cook dinner. We had seen many rabbits hit by cars but each time we stopped, they were already too cold or too flat to pickup and save for dinner. Ward drove a little slower for awhile and I unlimbered the shotgun. Managed to injure one on the second shot. I leaped out of the car and started off across a plowed field, flight boots sticking in the nearly frozen mud with each step. On the third step I was running in my stocking feet in the gunk. Th rabbit was injured and running almost slow enough for me to catch him without wasting another shell. Just as I got to him he took off like a shot and for what seemed like an eternity, I ran from one end of the plowed field to the other trying to corner the thing. Ward and the two girls were in the car laughing so loud I could hear them above the slurping of my now bare feet in the mud. The rabbit finally outmaneuvered me and ran towards the road. By this time I was so mad I crouched down and let fly with both barrels. Damn the expense of the shells! I missed the rabbit and blew the radiator ornament off the Buick. No more laughter. The rabbit ducked into a storm drain and was never seen again. Dejected, I slowly retraced my steps and picked up a

The ink in my forgery kit wouldn't work at this altitude, so we left.

sock here, a boot there, and slopped back to the car, where it took them at least half an hour to remove the mud from the botton half of me.

By now, it was so late we decided to cook right there beside the road. The dinner was well recieved, particularly after my recent cross country work out. Rather than drive all night, we drove only an hour or so until we were on the outskirts of a town. Still had to be close to a gas station so we could refill the radiator in the morning. I pulled off into a side road and Ward and I began to unload the junk in the trailer so we could climb into bed. By now the girls had given up pitching the tent every night and were sleeping in the front and back seat of the car. Sleeping there is o.k. but when you sleep on your back you are sitting up and when you roll over your feet are touching the back of your head. We all got to bed and were almost asleep when a diesel shifted gears about eight feet from the trailer. Diesel train, not truck. We were parked at the end of a train loading yard and all night long the switch engine would change direction near us. This didn't bother us after we got used to it; the bad thing was we were on the outside of a long curve after a 17 mile straightaway. The cars would roar into it like Fangio at Le Mans. Once, one came particulary close and I thought it was going right through us when it took off and went overhead. We were also parked at the end of the runway of an army air base and the whole air squadron was taking off at three minute intervals on a maneuver.

The following day, we took turns driving fifteen minutes each. By the time we got to Denver, we had almost made up for the loss of the night's sleep.

We bypassed Denver. . .too expensive. We went further south to Pike's Peak. You get there through Colorado Springs and The Broadmoor Country Club. Here we camped for the night. We chose the eleventh hole and were up and away before the first golfer made his round. Up the side of Pike's Peak now with the trailer in tow. I'll guarantee that we set no speed records of any kind. Nor did we even reach the summit. The tows were shut down for the season, so we left and coasted back down the side of this world famous mountain, to save money on gas.

North now and next stop. . . Berthoud Pass. At that time the total development was two rope tows. One on either side of the highway. An ancient surplus barracks (World War One). It housed some extremely enthusiastic people. They had an oil stove inside and offered us the heat that would be left over when the lights went out. Ward and I declined their offer but the girls took them up on it. We went back out and removed the debris, climbed into bed only to find that Ward's sleeping bag was stuck together with a bottle of poster paint that had broken and dribbled down into it. He shuffled together a half a suitcase of unpainted clothes and went back into the barracks building. There he donned everything that wasn't too small and curled up on the floor by the heater. As the night wore on and the cold of this altitude crept into the poorly insulated building, the heat of the stove began to diminish. In the morning, when I stumbled into the barracks, from the trailer, Ward was wrapped around the heater with all the clothes on, eight newspapers, a ski patrol tobaggon pad, wrappers from eighty-six packages of hot dog rolls, and a St. Bernard that stumbled in during the night.

The rope tows the following morning worked for awhile but the strength necessary to hold on at 10,000 feet above sea level makes a person soon get tired of the ski sport.

Next stop, Aspen. Enjoying its first, big time year with a gigantic lift, the world's longest for a single chair. Sneaking on was a problem that was not easy to cope with. We were tired, the gals were tired of us, so we parted ways. We deposited their luggage at the bottom of the lift and left for the West and Alta where we knew our way around a lot better.

Out of Glenwood Springs, just after sundown, the car in front of us hit a deer. At least I think it was the car in front of us because the deer was still warm. After much deliberation and the flavor of venison in our mouths, we decided against taking it. We couldn't afford the fine if we got caught with it in our possesion. Another dinner of kippered herring and oyster crackers and then to bed. This time we parked by a building in the town of Rifle, Colorado.

We disgorged all of the debris from inside the trailer and piled it in a heap on the ground. Next thing I knew, I heard voices. I opened my eyes and looked straight into a handlebar mustache. Shut them instantly. Nudged Ward and he mumbled something which resembled "GRUMPFFFXYTHESHERROFFFFFF." I opened one eye slyly and an old lady was peering at me. Shut again. Open again, three heads in the door now. People crowding around outside. Then everyone scattered as the zipper on my mummy bag began to move slowly. I got my head out of the bag and looked out . . . it was 11:30 on a Saturday morning and all of the ranchers were in town for their weekly shopping. We had parked in the middle of town and dumped all of our junk across the sidewalk

*We bought half a pound of hamburger, a box of crackers
and made a four and a half pound meat loaf.*

in front of the town's biggest store. Anyone who wanted to go anywhere had to climb over it, walk around it, and in general, swear at it.

We carried it off very well, however. We climbed out of bed, walked over and got our clothes out of the car. Then I climbed under the car and Ward started hammering on the engine with a wrench as if we had gotten stuck with engine trouble. When he finally finished hammering on it we really had a bit of trouble but nothing that some bubble gum and time wouldn't fix. We then shoveled the excess debris back into the car and went around to the back and started cooking breakfast. For a change, we had oatmeal. We offered some of it to the sheriff but he didn't like the raisins we had put in it. Too hard for him to gum, I guess.

Almost a week had gone by now without any fresh meat. We were motoring along just out of the town of Mack, Colorado when I saw my chance. A big bunch of chickens eating beside the road. I eased off onto the shoulder at 55 mph, the trailer bouncing like mad, when they heard me coming. I increased the angle of my veering off the road as they gathered momentum to get away from me. I finally nailed one about ten inches from the front porch of a farmer's house. It was only when I was climbing out of the car to retrieve it from the front bumper that I realized where I was. I couldn't get the door to the car open. It was up against the side of the house. Have you ever tried to back a trailer and car out of a front yard where you don't belong??? I dumped it into low, hoped for the best and spun a circle on the front lawn, bounced off the tractor, almost ran over the farmer's wife, who suddenly appeared from nowhere with a shotgun. We lucked out again 'cuz she tried to write down our license number instead of shooting at us.

We had learned a long time ago not to display our license unless asked by the police in a specific incident.

Cold cuts again for lunch. Definitely against them by now, Ward bought half a pound of hamburger, a box of crackers and made a four and a half pound meat loaf. We washed this down with gallons of cold water and lots of bread and peanut butter. Thus fortified, we drove westward.

Later in the afternoon, we stopped off at a place whose name we won't mention. They advertised "HOT STEAM-ING GEYSER ERUPTING EVERY HALF HOUR . . . Admission 25 cents." This seemed like a good cheap price for a shower, so we banged on the door to get admitted to see the geyser erupt. A sleepy degenerate brushed the flies away from the window and peered out through wine soaked eyes. Needing a shave ourselves, it took a bit of persuasion to get him to unlock the door and talk to us. We waved our 25 cents at him, then he asked about the bar of soap and towel we had along. Cost us ten cents more, but then imagine a scalding hot shower from a natural sulphur geyser for 35 cents. Natural isn't quite the word. It was a boiler from an abandoned LST that fell off a railroad train enroute from Tallahassee to San Francisco. Steam from the boiler is piped out into a pool. The valves are opened every half hour or whenever a crowd arrives. We had the place to ourselves for the eruption, so we soaped up in advance, lathered up for a shave and then our 35 cents only got us 17 seconds of geyser. It washed the soap down around our shoulders and then was turned off. The pool was only ankle deep so we were forced to lay down in it and roll over a couple of times to wash off the balance of the soap. I was waiting my turn to roll over in it when a car screeched to a halt outside and excited voices started hollering:

"It's them, I know it."

"Are your sure?'

"Who else would be driving a 1937 Buick convertible sedan with a trailer load of skis behind it and half of my prize hen buried in the front bumper?"

Caught!

We scrambled into our clothing and turned the geyser on. I held a piece of plywood over the nozzle so it would spray over the wall instead of straight up in the air. Ward looked through the crack in the fence and directed my aim. We completely inundated the sheriff and the farmer. They scrambled to get under cover, started their car, and tried to drive away. The yellow sulphur water covered the windows so they couldn't see out and seeped into the engine as the car slowly coughed to a stop. Held at bay by this yellow death, they couldn't get out of their car nor could they leave. Under cover of the water, Ward snuck out, started up our car and drove it around to the side. I propped a rock or two around the plywood so the geyser's angle of attack would remain constant and with the water coming down on the top of their car with such a loud noise that they couldn't hear us depart. We headed west and crossed the state line into Utah.

By now, it was spring in Utah. The deep powder that we had been used to in Alta was good, firm, corn snow. We got our jobs back working as fry cooks and snow shovelers at the Snow Pine Lodge. Again, we got our $10

Dawn came with an overcast sky and the smell of porcupine blood. . . .

a weekend and all we could eat. By this time our stomachs had shriveled a little so all we could eat wasn't half as much as it was in the fall. My pockets were still the same size however, and during the week for dinner every night, we still had our leftover hamburgers from the weekend.

About three nights later we were sleeping soundly when I heard something hissing. Sounded like someone getting a flat tire. In a place like this, who besides us had tires? I awoke half an hour later with the trailer leaning definitely to starboard. Ward had rolled over on top of me. I opened the door and he rolled right on out the door, sleeping bag and all, out into the snow on top of a porcupine who had just chewed a hole in our tire. Ward proceeded to beat him to death with a bagful of feathers and then climbed back into the trailer and went back to sleep.

Dawn came with an overcast sky and the smell of porcupine blood everywhere. Usually a porcupine will only eat the bark off the trees and he prefers Aspens to all else. This constant diet of tree bark gives them a bit of a gamey smell. More like a lumber yard in the hot sun. With the overcast sky, skiing was poor and the diet of hamburgers had about run its course. We decided to try and boil up a mess of porcupine stew and marinated porcupine hocks.

By lunch time, the odor of our cooking had drifted as far as The Alta Lodge and driven everyone closer to the bar. By three in the afternoon a fresh wind turned the drift in the other direction and the boiling pot was at the point of no return. We were both tired of melting snow to replenish that which had boiled away and the odor was

Spring—the deep snow was melting rapidly.

so bad we couldn't tell any longer whether or not it was the meat that smelled like aspens or the aspens that smelled like porcupine. I finally dumped in a whole box of pumpernickle seeds, some oregano, a smidgin' of sage, three pinches of pepper, some lima beans, half a thing of salt, two sweet potatoes, a tomato, four Idaho potatoes, a strip of bacon, some kippered herring to give it body, boiled the whole mess for another half or three quarters of an hour and then sat down to the best dog-gone dinner we had had in a long time. Oh, I can still taste those porcupine hocks and lima beans to this day.

The days now were getting long and warmer and the snow was melting rather rapidly. By now the snow was almost down to where it had been when we were there in the fall. I remembered some goat meat we had buried and lost in a blizzard in November. Ward and I started digging in the general vicinity of the place we had last seen it. Sure enough, there they were. An even half dozen Catalina goat meat chops. Ours for the cooking. Deeply frozen for the winter, they tasted as good as if we had lifted them out of our own deep freeze.

Of course, this sudden change of diet, porcupine, goat-meat, hamburger, from a steady diet of rabbits we had been eating, made us a little homesick. Then one morning a peculiar atmospheric phenomenon occurred at Alta that wound up the season for us. Alta is located just east of the Great Salt Lake desert and sometimes in the spring, the wind blows across the flats at 60 or 70 mph and raises great clouds of salt laden dust. This dust drifts east and settles on the deep snow pack in the Wasatch range. Nothing makes snow any stickier than salt. Everyone worked like mad to try and figure a wax combination of Fleer's double bubble, Dentyne, some hydrochloric acid and klister rubbed on lightly and blowtorched in. By the time I got my wax burnt onto my skis they were so hot the plastic top edges melted and ran down over the toe irons and I couldn't get my boots into them.

The following morning it had snowed three and a half inches over the salt and normal wax worked perfectly. This was too much. So we packed up and by night fall, started down the canyon. This time before we left, however, I checked all the lugnuts personally for a loose one. They were all on tight so the trip seemed destined to go off as planned. We got the car all packed, and started the engine. I changed from my ski boots to my flight boots, or boot. I stomped down in one and squashed the life out of a poor little field mouse who had found a warm home in out of the snow.

Driving down the winding, narrow road we were again trying to get to a gas station without running the engine too much when the throttle stuck. I turned the ignition key off and the gasoline that remained in the pistons must have blown out all at the same time. With a gigantic roar it all exploded in the muffler. Blowing parts all over the highway. I turned the ignition on in hopes that we could still salvage what was left of the car without another explosion. Belching smoke, like a Mitsubachi 109 over Okinawa, we skidded and roared down the canyon. By this time Ward was hiding on the floor under the dash.

"Hold the steering wheel, I'll try and unjam the throttle", I hollered. I bent over to unjam the throttle and there were two hands there already working on it. Mine made four. There were two of us in the car.

Who was steering?

No one.

The road curved in just the right place for us, twice, before I got the clutch in and the thing slowed down a little. Afraid to turn off the ignition key again, for fear of a more disastrous explosion, I tried to bring the machinery to a halt on the steep hill with only the brakes. They slowed it down to about 48 or 49 mph when they started to heat up and locked. With all four wheels skidding on the ice and the trailer slowly turning sideways to pass us, I hoped for only one thing. Asphalt. I got my wish in about fifteen feet. The car stopped in about 30 feet while spewing all the debris form the back seat all over me and more all over Ward. Somehow the car managed to keep from skidding sideways but when the dust and debris settled, Ward was lodged under that dashboard tighter than Aunt Fanny in her new mail order corset. Right in the middle of the road we sat. All four wheels locked with bonded brakes. With the trailer out beside us we couldn't let a car go by in either direction nor could we get a shove. Before the brakes cooled off enough to release, we had about thirty cars backed up in one direction and fourteen in the other.

Fortunately, we had enough stew left over to heat up and give everyone a snack while they were waiting. Two girls even asked for the recipe. We told them "it was something we had whipped up from some leftovers the other night." Which was true. . . leftover porcupine. One of the people, whose car we were holding up, had a couple of gallons of wine left over after a day of skiing and the thing was just generating into a first class type party when a big-blade snow plow came down the hill. The driver was late for dinner and so he eased by the line of cars, pushed his big blade up against the side of the car

. . .we put the lid back on the porcupine squeezin's. . .

and trailer and slid it over to the side of the road so he could get by. This kind of took the edge of the party and everyone slowly went on home. We put the lid back on the few remaining tidbits of porcupine squeezings and turned on the radio and waited.

The tubes warmed up at the same time the brakes cooled off enough to allow the car to move. We coasted on down into hearing distance of the local station. Again, this hissing sound. I know porcupines wouldn't run as fast as we were now coasting, when the windshield began to fog up.

This time the radiator in the car heater had frozen and broken. A hot jet of steam was shooting all over the front seat. Ward had escaped to the back and there he sat. Midst the debris of seven months of skiing; old pop bottles, dirty sox, etc.

Why?

"To glide effortlessly down steep mountains, carving graceful arcs of ecstasy in the deep powder snow."

Which is what we had been doing.

*Why? "To glide effortlessly down steep mountains,
carving graceful arcs of ecstasy
in the deep powder snow."*

Still 750 miles from Los Angeles, as the crow flies, but about twice as far as the Buick drives, we took stock of our financial situation. We had left home on the 13th of November and it was now the 16th of April. This was a ski vacation of 154 days. Our total expenses for the trip including gas, food, lodging (????), shotgun shells, tapioca, and a fine of ten dollars in Elko, Nevada, came to $268.00. Of this amount, we squandered $18.00 of it in Sun Valley, Idaho. Those were the days when you could ski anywhere for less than a dollar a day. Now you spend four dollars phoning for reservations. Not me. I still have a small trailer, buy oyster crackers wholesale, ketchup by the gallon, and am the only home owner in our subdivision who raises rabbits in the basement.

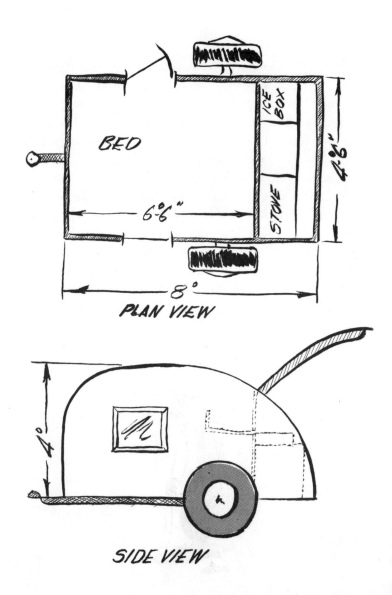

ICE BOX

BED

STOVE

6'-6"

4'-8"

8°

PLAN VIEW

4°

SIDE VIEW

Architectural rendering of
Miller's Mobile Mansion.

*Moving from parking lot to parking lot at almost
every ski resort from Yosemite to Aspen during
the winter of 1946/47, Warren Miller and Ward
Baker have been going downhill ever since.*

*Ward Baker comes in for a landing after
executing a difficult terrain jump.
Terrain jumps were necessary because
there was no snowgrooming in 1947.*

*Warren attempts a parallel christie on the
side of Dollar Mountain at Sun Valley, Idaho.
The day this picture was taken it was easier
to sneak on the lift on Dollar Mountain than
it was to sneak on the lift on Baldy.*

*Living on rabbits, oyster crackers and
ketchup, the team set records in 1946/47
that will never be broken*

When the Buick broke down in Las Vegas,
they fixed it in the parking lot of the
combination casino, dance hall, convenience
store, gift shop, pool hall, sporting
goods store, garage, gas station and motel.

When Ward Baker and I returned to Badger Pass where our first ski trip together really started in 1945, I began to thaw out in the warm California sun and started to once again draw my pencil cartoons of a day's event, put them up on the bulletin board and sell them for a dollar. We returned to Yosemite with about an hour of 8mm movies that we had taken on our winter-long trip. The Winter Sports Director at Badger Pass, Bill Janss arranged for us to show them in the lobby of The Awahnee Hotel. Apparently what we had been doing all winter was so preposterous and dumb, that the twenty or twenty-five people laughed at almost every scene we showed and narrated. They had to believe our stories because we had movies to prove them. Movies of frozen rabbits, living in the parking lot at Sun Valley and Alta, and doing anything that a some-what abnormal, couple of ski-bums would do while sleeping in an unheated trailer and skiing seven days a week.

That first 8mm film show was the start of a fifty-year long career of sports film production and I'm look-ing forward to the next fifty years.

Warren drew cartoons and sold them for a dollar each to help defer the high cost of the ski vacation.

Lithographs of Warren's Original Drawings

Jack Reddish, from Salt Lake City, was on the 1948 U.S. Olympic team and in 1950 won the National Slalom Championship by eight seconds and was seventeen seconds ahead of the third place finisher. He went on to work in Hollywood. **$300**

Warren Miller when he still had hair and was teaching skiing at Sun Valley, Idaho. Warren has produced over five hundred sports films during his fifty-year career of lurching from one near-disaster to the next as he wandered the world with his camera. He refuses to retire. **$450**

Leon Goodman taught skiing at Sun Valley, Idaho, for many years until he moved to a small town in Northern Idaho where he owned and managed a bowling alley until retiring in McCall, Idaho. **$300**

These 16" x 20" pen and ink drawings were made after the Harriman Cup in Sun Valley, Idaho, in 1948. Warren drew the originals on a dining room table in the Challenger Inn when he was living in the nearby parking lot. They have been lithographed in a limited edition of five hundred and each one is hand painted, numbered, signed, and framed. Each lithograph can be individually autographed by Warren to the purchaser or anyone they designate.

Any one of these lithographs, or the set of five, will make a great gift for the people who have loaned you their condominium for your annual ski vacation; or hang them in your office so you can be reminded of why you work so hard. Warren will personally autograph them to you or the person of your choice.

For a color brochure of these lithographs please contact:
Mac Productions
Fax: 425.844.9245 or
Email: mac.productions@gte.net

Barney McLean, was the captain of the 1948 Olympic Ski Team in St. Moritz. He started his career as a nordic ski jumper and his experience at high speeds in the air helped him become one of America's most successful ski racers. He enjoyed a long career in the ski industry and is now retired. $300

Toni Matt was born and raised in Austria and came to America to teach skiing for Hannes Schneider at North Conway, New Hampshire, in the mid 1930's. He achieved instant fame when he skied straight down the headwall at Tuckerman's Ravine. He spent many years skiing at North Conway. $300

SELECTIONS OF WARREN MILLER BOOKS

"You have enjoyed his ski movies for years. Now enjoy his hilarious books about those years"

ON FILM IN PRINT

Warren has been skiing and surfing since 1937 and has spent most of the last fifty years on the road with his camera and skis, boats and windsurfers, while chasing freedom, finding it, filming it, or writing about it. This is a collection of almost fifty short stories about his unusual lifestyle while traveling the world from New Zealand to Zermatt, from Malibu to Maui and a lot of other places in between.

ITEM #301 Soft Cover $12.95
ITEM #302 Hard Cover $24.95

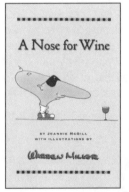

A NOSE FOR WINE

Warren's irreverent cartoon illustrations of winespeak. 'Great legs,' 'Tannin,' 'A hint of bitterness,' ' Well proportioned,' are just a few of the misunderstood wine terms that are explained by Jeannie McGill and humorously illustrated by Warren.

ITEM #601 Hard Cover $19.95

WINE, WOMEN, WARREN, AND SKIS

The hilarious saga of Warren's six month ski trip during the winter of '46-'47 while living on oyster crackers and ketchup, frozen rabbits, poached ducks, goat meat, and powder snow. He slept in an eight-foot-long-trailer at eight-below-zero in the parking lots in the finest ski resorts in the west. Learn how to ski for a hundred days in Sun Valley, Idaho for only $18 or at Alta, Utah for $2.50 a week. And there are a lot of antique photos to prove it.

ITEM #501 Soft Cover $11.95

SKI AND SNOW COUNTRY

120 brilliant black and white photographs by Ray Atkeson from the 1940's and 50's with essay and captions by Warren Miller. Almost everyone in the book was a friend of Warren's so he wrote the essay and the book the same way he used to narrate his movies, with a combination of nostalgia, reportage, and humor. For anyone who skied or had a friend or relative, who skied in the formative years of the sport, this is a coffee table book designed for you.

ITEM #201 Hard Cover $23.95

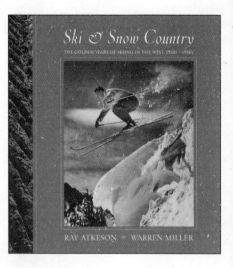

LURCHING FROM ONE NEAR DISASTER TO THE NEXT

A collection of fifty short stories from the last fifty years of Warren lurching through life. The Truck from Hell, Golf Anyone, The Whirlpool, Swimming with the Whales are just some of the classic stories in this, the latest collection of stories about Warren's unique lifestyle.

ITEM #401 Soft Cover $14.95
ITEM #402 Hard Cover $24.95

"If you don't do it this year,

you